Collins

Very First
French
Words

HarperCollins Publishers
Westerhill Road
Bishopbriggs
Glasgow
G64 2QT

First edition 2012

Reprint 10 9 8 7 6 5 4 3 2 1 0

© HarperCollins Publishers 2012

ISBN 978-0-00-744747-3

Collins ® is a registered trademark of
HarperCollins Publishers Limited

www.collinslanguage.com

A catalogue record for this book is available
from the British Library

Printed by Imago in China

Audio recorded and produced by
www.tomdickanddebbie.com

Artwork and design by Q2AMedia

Content developed and compiled by
Karen Jamieson

Project Management by Anna Stevenson

Translation by Lola Busuttil

For the publisher:
Gaëlle Amiot-Cadey
Lucy Cooper
Kerry Ferguson
Elaine Higgleton
Lisa Sutherland

This book includes a CD of French words and phrases. The tracks on the CD are:

Contents

Welcome to France!
Bienvenue en France!

What's your name?
Comment tu t'appelles?

My name is Claire.
Je m'appelle Claire.

Hello!
Bonjour!

Hello!
Bonjour!

Thank you.
Merci.

You're welcome.
De rien.

Goodbye!
Au revoir!

Goodbye!
Au revoir!

Did you know?

When French children lose a tooth, they put it under their pillow and the tooth mouse (la petite souris) takes it and leaves a coin in its place.

Did you know?

On Twelfth Night families eat la galette des Rois, a pastry cake. Whoever finds the lucky token (la fève) inside is declared king or queen and given a crown.

the Eiffel Tower
la tour Eiffel

the Tour de France
le Tour de France

the 14th of July
le quatorze juillet

the Alps
les Alpes

Did you know?

The Eiffel Tower took two years to build and was finished in 1889. It is 324 metres tall, with nearly 1700 steps and a lift that go all the way up to the top!

Did you know?

The 14th of July is France's national day: on this day in 1789 the French Revolution began. People enjoy celebrating with fireworks, parades and dancing.

My family
Ma famille

grandpa
le grand-père

grandma
la grand-mère

Activities

1. Find the hidden parrot.
2. Who lives with you?

brother
le frère

4

mummy
la maman

daddy
le papa

me
moi

sister
la sœur

My pets
Mes animaux de compagnie

hamster
le hamster

kitten
le chaton

guinea pig
le cochon d'Inde

Activities

1. Find the hidden umbrella.
2. Can you hop like a rabbit and stretch like a cat?

tortoise
la tortue

6

rabbit
le lapin

cat
le chat

puppy
le chiot

dog
le chien

My day
Ma journée

I get up.
Je me lève.

I get dressed.
Je m'habille.

I go to school.
Je vais à l'école.

I play.
Je joue.

Activities

1. Find the hidden kangaroo.
2. What have you done today?

I have a snack.
Je prends mon goûter.

8

I listen to a story.
J'écoute une histoire.

I go home.
Je vais à la maison.

I have a bath.
Je prends un bain.

I go to bed.
Je vais au lit.

The weather
Le temps qu'il fait

It's rainy.
Il pleut.

It's snowy.
Il y a de la neige.

It's sunny.
Il fait soleil.

It's windy.
Il fait du vent.

Activities

1. Find the hidden tiger.
2. What's the weather like today?

It's cloudy.
Il y a des nuages.

It's hot.
Il fait chaud.

It's cold.
Il fait froid.

It's stormy.
Il y a de l'orage.

My body and face
Mon corps et mon visage

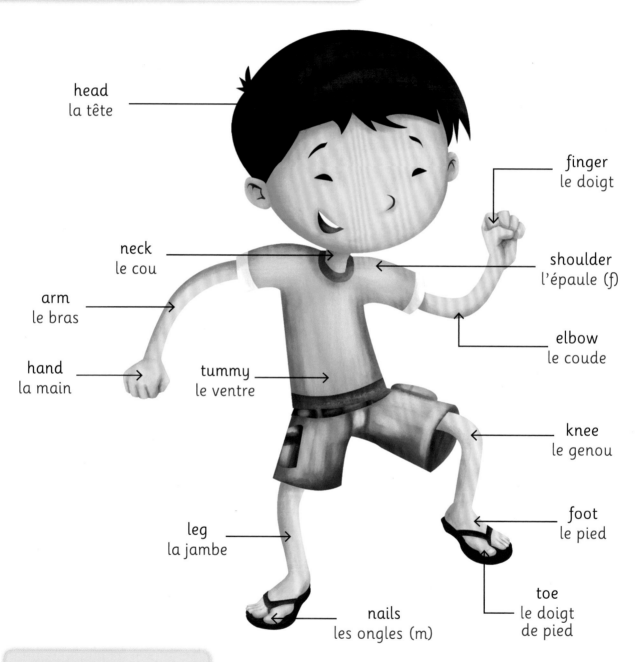

head
la tête

finger
le doigt

neck
le cou

shoulder
l'épaule (f)

arm
le bras

elbow
le coude

hand
la main

tummy
le ventre

knee
le genou

foot
le pied

leg
la jambe

toe
le doigt
de pied

nails
les ongles (m)

Activities

1. Can you pat your head and rub your tummy?
2. Can you touch your toes?

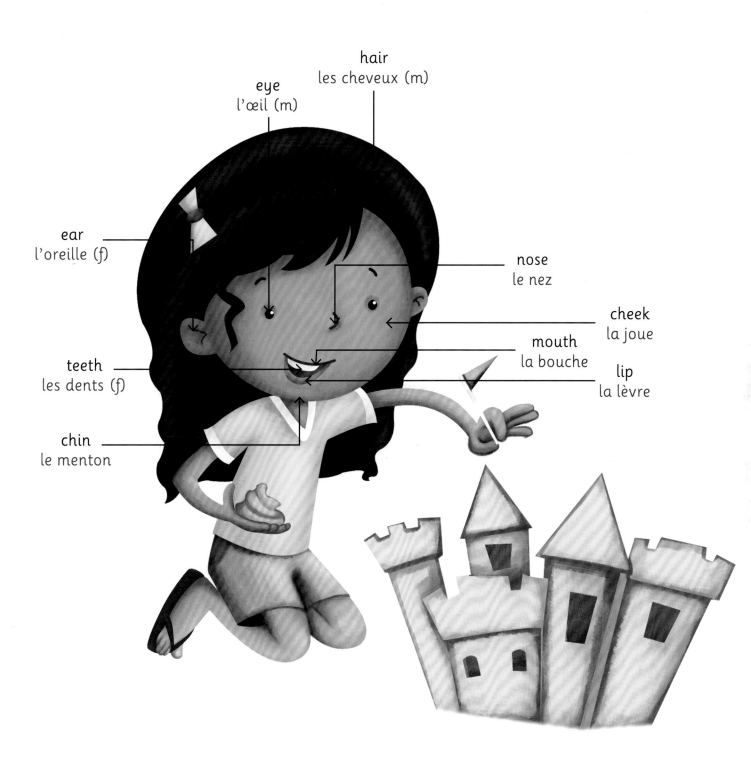

eye
l'œil (m)

hair
les cheveux (m)

ear
l'oreille (f)

nose
le nez

cheek
la joue

mouth
la bouche

teeth
les dents (f)

lip
la lèvre

chin
le menton

How I feel
Comment je me sens

I'm angry.
Je suis en colère.

I'm sad.
Je suis triste.

I'm happy.
Je suis contente.

I'm tired.
Je suis fatiguée.

Activities

1. Find the hidden apple.
2. How do you feel today?

I'm hungry.
J'ai faim.

I'm thirsty.
J'ai soif.

I'm scared.
J'ai peur.

I'm shy.
Je suis timide.

Things I do
Ce que je fais

I stand up.
Je me lève.

I sit down.
Je m'assois.

I touch my toes.
Je touche mes orteils.

I jump.
Je saute.

Activities

1. Find the hidden teddy.
2. Mime some of these actions.

16

I eat.
Je mange.

I drink.
Je bois.

I cry.
Je pleure.

I laugh.
Je ris.

More things I do
D'autres choses que je fais

I hold my daddy's hand.
Je donne la main
à mon papa.

I wave.
Je fais un signe
de la main.

I run.
Je cours.

I walk.
Je marche.

Activities

1. Find the hidden shell.
2. Can you make a noise like a monkey?

18

I clap.
J'applaudis.

I dance.
Je danse.

I sing.
Je chante.

I make a circle.
Je fais la ronde.

I can count
Je sais compter

1 un

2 deux

3 trois

4 quatre

5 cinq

Activities

1. Can you count to 10?
2. How many cars can you see in the picture?

6 six

7 sept

8 huit

9 neuf

10 dix

Colours
Les couleurs

white
blanc

green
vert

blue
bleu

Activities

1. Find the hidden snake.
2. Find all the colours in the picture.

purple
violet

black
noir

brown
marron

grey
gris

pink
rose

red
rouge

yellow
jaune

orange
orange

Summer clothes
Habits d'été

skirt
la jupe

shirt
la chemise

T-shirt
le tee-shirt

Activities

1. Find the hidden trumpet.
2. What do you wear in summer?

swimming
trunks
le caleçon

swimsuit
le maillot
de bain

shorts
le short

sandals
les sandales (f)

dress
la robe

sunglasses
les lunettes de soleil (f)

sun hat
le chapeau de soleil

25

Winter clothes
Habits d'hiver

jacket
le blouson

boots
les bottes (f)

Activities

1. Find the hidden bicycle.
2. What do you wear in winter?

gloves
les gants (m)

scarf
l'écharpe (f)

coat
le manteau

trousers
le pantalon

jeans
le jean

shoes
les chaussures (f)

hat
le bonnet

sweatshirt
le sweat

My classroom
Ma salle de classe

teacher
la maîtresse

computer
l'ordinateur (m)

girl
la fille

Activities

1. Find the hidden birthday cake.
2. How many children are in the picture?

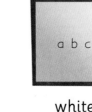

whiteboard
le tableau

schoolbag
le sac à dos

toys
les jouets (m)

poster
l'affiche (f)

bookcase
la bibliothèque

boy
le garçon

book
le livre

chair
la chaise

table
la table

pencil case
la trousse

Fast or slow?
Rapide ou lent?

rabbit
le lapin

slow | fast
lent | rapide

tortoise
la tortue

small | big
petit | grand

Activities

1. Find the hidden train.
2. Can you move slowly like a tortoise and fast like a rabbit?

hippo
l'hippopotame (m)

strong | weak
fort | faible

gorilla
le gorille

dirty | clean
sale | propre

monkey
le singe

elephant
l'éléphant (m)

Find the shapes
Trouve les formes

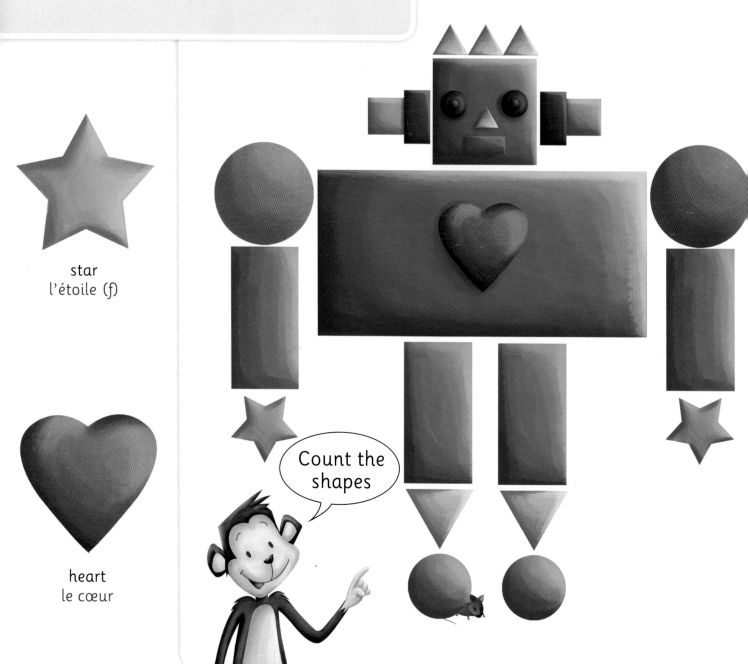

star
l'étoile (f)

heart
le cœur

Count the
shapes

rectangle
le rectangle

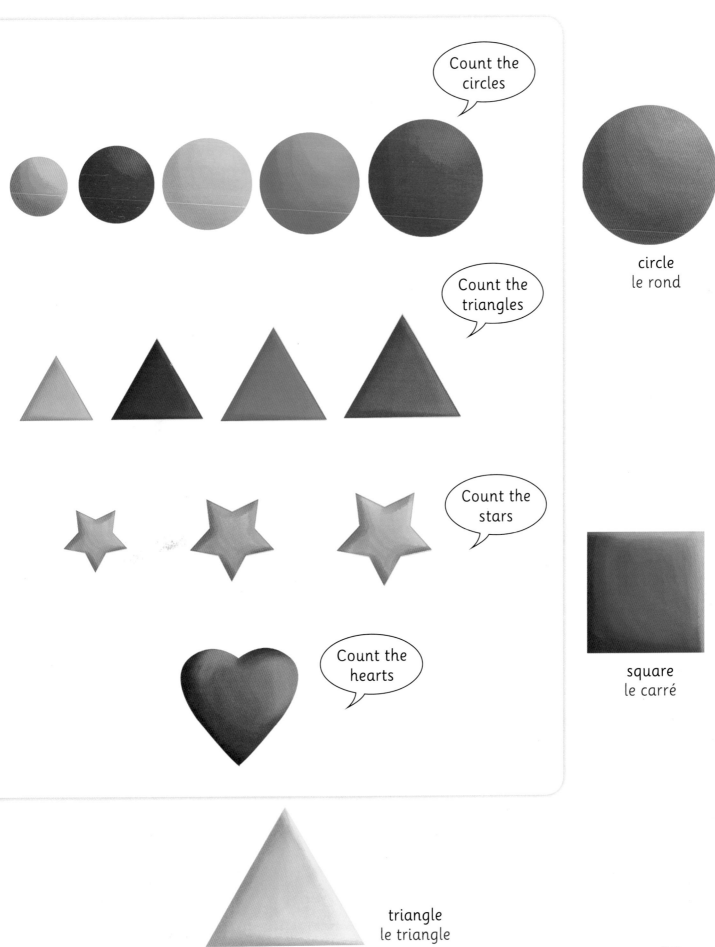

Count the circles

Count the triangles

Count the stars

Count the hearts

circle
le rond

square
le carré

triangle
le triangle

33

In the sea
Dans la mer

dolphin
le dauphin

octopus
la pieuvre

seal
le phoque

Activities

1. Find the hidden schoolbag.
2. How many fish can you see in the picture?

shark
le requin

fish
le poisson

turtle
la tortue
de mer

walrus
le morse

whale
la baleine

penguin
le pingouin

On the farm
À la ferme

farmer
le fermier

straw
la paille

chicken
la poule

Activities

1. Find the hidden octopus.
2. Can you make farm animal noises?

donkey
l'âne (m)

goose
l'oie (f)

sheep
le mouton

mouse
la souris

rat
le rat

duck
le canard

cow
la vache

horse
le cheval

Animal Olympics
Animaux en compétition

baboon
le babouin

crocodile
le crocodile

Activities

1. Find the hidden hat.
2. Which animal do you like best?

elephant
l'éléphant (m)

zebra
le zèbre

giraffe
la girafe

rhino
le rhinocéros

hippo
l'hippopotame (m)

lion
le lion

cheetah
le guépard

39

Seaside dance
Bal au fond de l'océan

shell
le coquillage

starfish
l'étoile de mer (f)

Activities

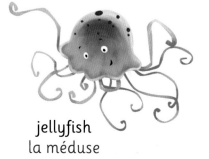

1. Find the hidden spoon.
2. Can you pretend to be a starfish?

jellyfish
la méduse

seahorse
l'hippocampe (m)

seaweed
les algues (f)

crab
le crabe

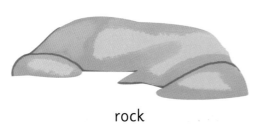

rock
le rocher

fish
le poisson

At the castle
Au château

princess
la princesse

prince
le prince

dragon
le dragon

Activities

1. Find the hidden crab.
2. Can you roar like a dragon?

castle
le château

crown
la couronne

musician
le musicien

knight
le chevalier

flag
le drapeau

king
le roi

queen
la reine

Jungle football
Football dans la jungle

monkey
le singe

chimpanzee
le chimpanzé

snake
le serpent

Activities

1. Find the hidden drum.
2. Can you slither like a snake?

tiger
le tigre

gorilla
le gorille

parrot
le perroquet

orangutan
l'orang-outan (m)

lizard
le lézard

leopard
le léopard

45

Bugs and mini beasts
Petites bestioles

bee
l'abeille (f)

butterfly
le papillon

Activities

1. Find the hidden bananas.
2. Can you buzz like a bee?

ladybird
la coccinelle

grasshopper
la sauterelle

ant
la fourmi

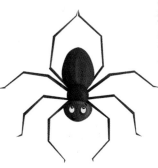

spider
l'araignée (f)

beetle
le scarabée

caterpillar
la chenille

My birthday party
Ma fête d'anniversaire

birthday present
le cadeau
d'anniversaire

birthday card
la carte
d'anniversaire

ice cream
la glace

Activities

1. Find the hidden bee.
2. Can you count the candles on the cake?

balloon
le ballon

birthday cake
le gâteau
d'anniversaire

candle
la bougie

fruit
les fruits (m)

friend
la copine

friend
le copain

sandwiches
les sandwichs (m)

popcorn
le pop-corn

sweets
les bonbons (m)

water
l'eau (f)

Breakfast time
L'heure du petit déjeuner

toast
la tartine grillée

coffee
le café

| tea | cup |
| le thé | la tasse |

Activities

1. Find the hidden paintbrush.
2. What do you have for breakfast?

yoghurt
le yaourt

spoon
la cuillère

glass
le verre

honey
le miel

juice
le jus de fruits

jam
la confiture

cereal
les céréales (f)

milk
le lait

bread
le pain

knife
le couteau

My town
Ma ville

swimming pool
la piscine

hairdresser's
le coiffeur

library
la bibliothèque

school
l'école (f)

Activities

1. Find the hidden chimpanzee.
2. Which of these things have you seen in your town?

car
la voiture

doctor's
le médecin

road
la rue

playground
la cour de
récréation

motorbike
la moto

toy shop
le magasin
de jouets

supermarket
le supermarché

dentist's
le dentiste

bus
le bus

At the park
Au parc

lake
le lac

bicycle
la bicyclette

kite
le cerf-volant

ball
le ballon

Activities

1. Find the hidden tortoise.
2. Do you like to play at the park?

boat
la barque

seesaw
le tape-cul

tree
l'arbre (m)

bin
la poubelle

slide
le toboggan

bird
l'oiseau (m)

scooter
la trottinette

swing
la balançoire

climbing frame
la structure

At the supermarket
Au supermarché

lettuce
la laitue

mushroom
le champignon

carrot
la carotte

Activities

1. Find the hidden train.
2. Which vegetables do you like best?

potato
la pomme
de terre

broccoli
les brocolis (m)

basket
le panier

tomato
la tomate

cucumber
le concombre

red pepper
le poivron rouge

onion
l'oignon (m)

green pepper
le poivron vert

The fruit stall
Chez le marchand de fruits

watermelon
la pastèque

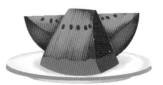

pear
la poire

pineapple
l'ananas (m)

Activities

1. Find the hidden seahorse.
2. What is your favourite fruit?

orange
l'orange (f)

strawberry
la fraise

banana
la banane

peach
la pêche

apple
la pomme

grapes
le raisin

cherry
la cerise

In the kitchen
Dans la cuisine

butter
le beurre

scales
la balance

flour
la farine

Activities

1. Find the hidden sunglasses.
2. Do you like to help in the kitchen?

plate
l'assiette (f)

honey
le miel

egg
l'œuf (m)

sugar
le sucre

bowl
le saladier

spoon
la cuillère

whisk
le fouet

oven
le four

biscuit
le biscuit

A special dinner
Un dîner spécial

knife
le couteau

rice
le riz

fork
la fourchette

pepper
le poivre

Activities

1. Find the hidden flower.
2. What do you like to eat for dinner?

steak
le steak

peas
les petits
pois (m)

ketchup
le ketchup

salad
la salade

soup
la soupe

fish
le poisson

salt
le sel

hamburger
le hamburger | chips
les frites (f)

potato
la pomme
de terre | beans
les haricots
blancs (m)

At bedtime
Avant d'aller au dodo

I dry myself.
Je me sèche.

towel
la serviette

I have a shower.
Je prends une douche.

I put on my pyjamas.
Je mets mon pyjama.

teddy bear
l'ours en peluche (m)

I brush my teeth.
Je me brosse les dents.

I brush my hair.
Je me coiffe.

Activities

1. Find the hidden cat.
2. What time do you go to bed?

bed
le lit

I go to the toilet.
Je vais aux toilettes.

I wash my hands.
Je me lave les mains.

pyjamas
le pyjama

I get into bed.
Je me mets au lit.

mirror
le miroir

I kiss my teddy.
J'embrasse mon ours en peluche.

I say goodnight.
Je dis bonne nuit.

toothpaste
le dentifrice

toothbrush
la brosse à dents

Art
Activités artistiques

paper
le papier

glue
la colle

Activities

1. Find the hidden rabbit.
2. How many pencils are on the table?

crayon
le crayon gras

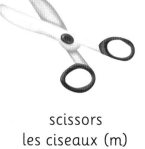

scissors
les ciseaux (m)

pencil
le crayon

marker
le feutre

paint
la peinture

brush
le pinceau

Music
Musique

triangle
le triangle

guitar
la guitare

Activities

1. Find the hidden pair of scissors.
2. Mime playing one of the instruments.

keyboard
le clavier

68

tambourine
le tambourin

trumpet
la trompette

drum
le tambour

xylophone
le xylophone

violin
le violon

69

Let's play!
Allons jouer!

ball
le ballon

bricks
les Lego® (m)

fire engine
le camion de
pompiers

Activities

1. Find the hidden duck.
2. What is your favourite toy?

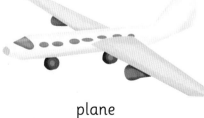

plane
l'avion (m)

train
le train

70

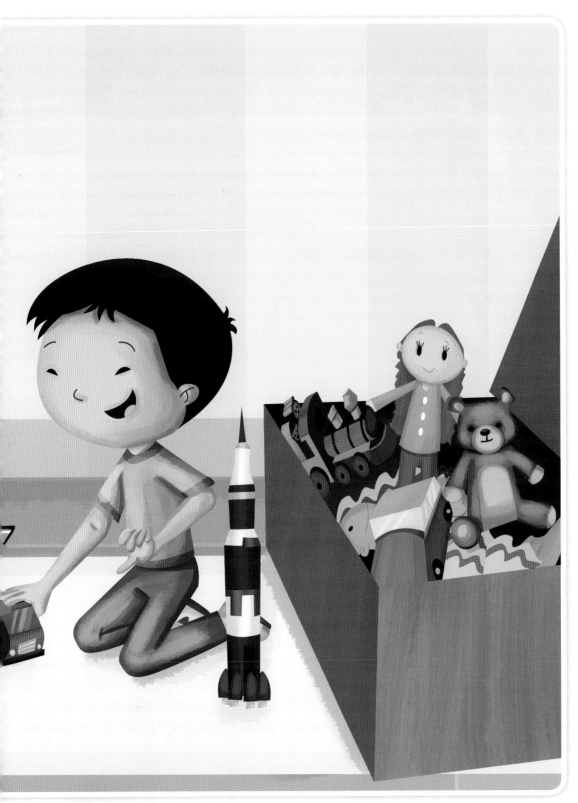

rocket
la fusée

doll
la poupée

toy box
le coffre à jouets

teddy bear
l'ours en peluche (m)

puzzle
le puzzle

71

Food in France
La nourriture en France

ham
le jambon

chicken and
fried potatoes
le poulet et les
pommes de
terre sautées

ham and
cheese toastie
le croque-monsieur

sponge cake
la madeleine

At school
À l'école

Activities

1. Find the hidden flower.
2. Which of these foods would you like to try?

tuna sandwich
le sandwich
au thon

green beans
les haricots
verts (m)

72

beef stew
le pot au feu

pasta
les pâtes (f)

salad
la salade

At home
À la maison

French toast
le pain perdu

apple tart
la tarte aux
pommes

cheese
le fromage

Words and phrases
Mots et expressions

m = masculine; f = feminine; pl = plural in French only; sing = singular in French only

A, a

Alps Alpes f
angry: I'm angry. Je suis
    en colère.
animal animal m
ant fourmi f
apple pomme f
apple tart tarte aux pommes f
arm bras m
art activités artistiques f pl

B, b

baboon babouin m
ball ballon m
balloon ballon m
banana banane f
basket panier m
bath: I have a bath. Je prends
    un bain.
beans haricots blancs m
bed lit m; I get into bed. Je me
    mets au lit. I go to bed.
    Je vais au lit.
bee abeille f
beef stew pot au feu m
beetle scarabée m
bicycle bicyclette f
big grand
bin poubelle f
bird oiseau m
birthday anniversaire m
birthday cake gâteau
    d'anniversaire m
birthday card carte
    d'anniversaire f
birthday party fête
    d'anniversaire f
birthday present cadeau
    d'anniversaire m
biscuit biscuit m
black noir
blue bleu
boat barque f

body corps m
book livre m
bookcase bibliothèque f
boots bottes f
bowl saladier m
boy garçon m
bread pain m
breakfast petit déjeuner m
bricks Lego® m
broccoli brocolis m pl
brother frère m
brown marron
brush pinceau m
bus bus m
butter beurre m
butterfly papillon m

C, c

candle bougie f
car voiture f
carrot carotte f
castle château m
cat chat m
caterpillar chenille f
cereal céréales f pl
chair chaise f
cheese fromage m
cheetah guépard m
cherry cerise f
chicken (bird) poule f
chicken (meat) poulet m
chimpanzee chimpanzé m
chin menton m
chips frites f
circle rond m; I make a circle.
    Je fais la ronde.
clap: I clap. J'applaudis.
classroom salle de classe f
clean propre
climbing frame structure f
clothes habits m
cloudy: It's cloudy. Il y a
    des nuages.

74

coat manteau m
coffee café m
cold: It's cold. Il fait froid.
colour couleur f
computer ordinateur m
cow vache f
crab crabe m
crayon crayon gras m
crocodile crocodile m
crown couronne f
cry: I cry. Je pleure.
cucumber concombre m
cup tasse f

D, d
daddy papa m
dance: I dance. Je danse.
day journée f
dentist dentiste m
dinner dîner m
dirty sale
doctor médecin m
dog chien m
doll poupée f
dolphin dauphin m
donkey âne m
dragon dragon m
dress robe f
dressed: I get dressed. Je
    m'habille.
drink: I drink. Je bois.
drum tambour m
dry: I dry myself. Je me sèche.
duck canard m

E, e
ear oreille f
eat: I eat. Je mange.
egg œuf m
Eiffel Tower tour Eiffel f
eight huit
elephant éléphant m
eye œil (eyes = yeux) m

F, f
face visage m
family famille f
farm ferme f
farmer fermier m

fast rapide
finger doigt m
fire engine camion de pompiers m
fish poisson m
five cinq
flag drapeau m
flour farine f
foot pied m
football football m
fork fourchette f
four quatre
France France f
French toast pain perdu m
fried potatoes pommes de terre
    sautées f
friend (boy) copain m
friend (girl) copine f
fruit fruits m pl

G, g
get up: I get up. Je me lève.
giraffe girafe f
girl fille f
glass verre m
gloves gants m
glue colle f
go: I go to school Je vais à l'école.
    I go home. Je vais à la maison.
goose oie f
gorilla gorille m
grandma grand-mère f
grandpa grand-père m
grapes raisin m sing
grasshopper sauterelle f
green vert
green beans haricots verts m
green pepper poivron vert m
grey gris
guinea pig cochon d'Inde m
guitar guitare f

H, h
hair cheveux m; I brush my hair.
    Je me coiffe.
hairdresser coiffeur m
ham jambon m
ham and cheese toastie
    croque-monsieur m

hamburger hamburger m
hamster hamster m
hand main f
happy: I'm happy. Je suis contente.
hat bonnet m
head tête f
heart cœur m
hippo hippopotame m
hold: I hold my daddy's hand. Je
    donne la main à mon papa.
honey miel m
horse cheval m
hot: It's hot. Il fait chaud.
hungry: I'm hungry. J'ai faim.

I, i

ice cream glace f

J, j

jacket blouson m
jam confiture f
jeans jean m sing
jellyfish méduse f
juice jus de fruits m
jump: I jump. Je saute.
jungle jungle f

K, k

ketchup ketchup m
keyboard clavier m
king roi m
kiss: I kiss my teddy. J'embrasse
    mon ours en peluche.
kitchen cuisine f
kite cerf-volant m
kitten chaton m
knee genou m
knife couteau m
knight chevalier m

L, l

ladybird coccinelle f
lake lac m
laugh: I laugh. Je ris.
leg jambe f
leopard léopard m
lettuce laitue f
library bibliothèque f
lion lion m
lip lèvre f

listen: I listen to a story. J'écoute
    une histoire.
lizard lézard m

M, m

marker feutre m
me moi
milk lait m
mirror miroir m
monkey singe m
motorbike moto f
mouse souris f
mouth bouche f
mummy maman f
mushroom champignon m
music musique f
musician musicien m

N, n

nails ongles m
neck cou m
nine neuf
nose nez m

O, o

octopus pieuvre f
one un
onion oignon m
orange (colour) orange
orange (fruit) orange f
orangutan orang-outan m
oven four m

P, p

paint peinture f
paper papier m
park parc m
parrot perroquet m
pasta pâtes f pl
peach pêche f
pear poire f
peas petits pois m
pencil crayon m
pencil case trousse f
penguin pingouin m
pepper poivre m
pet animal de compagnie m
pineapple ananas m
pink rose
plane avion m

plate assiette f
play: I play. Je joue.
playground cour de récréation f
popcorn pop-corn m
poster affiche f
potato pomme de terre f
prince prince m
princess princesse f
puppy chiot m
purple violet
put on: I put on my pyjamas. Je
    mets mon pyjama.
puzzle puzzle m
pyjamas pyjama m sing

Q, q
queen reine f

R, r
rabbit lapin m
rainy: It's rainy. Il pleut.
rat rat m
rectangle rectangle m
red rouge
red pepper poivron rouge m
rhino rhinocéros m
rice riz m
road rue f
rock rocher m
rocket fusée f
ruler règle f
run: I run. Je cours.

S, s
sad: I'm sad. Je suis triste.
salad salade f
salt sel m
sandals sandales f
sandcastle château de sable m
sandwiches sandwiches m
scales balance f
scared: I'm scared. J'ai peur.
scarf écharpe f
school école f
schoolbag sac à dos m
scissors ciseaux m
scooter trottinette f
seahorse hippocampe m
sea mer f
seal phoque m

seaweed algues f pl
seesaw tape-cul m
seven sept
shape forme f
shark requin m
sheep mouton m
shell coquillage m
shirt chemise f
shoes chaussures f
shorts short m sing
shoulder épaule f
shower: I have a shower. Je prends
    une douche.
shy: I'm shy. Je suis timide.
sing: I sing. Je chante.
sister sœur f
sit down: I sit down. Je m'assois.
six six
skirt jupe f
slide toboggan m
slow lent
small petit
snack: I have a snack. Je prends
    mon goûter.
snake serpent m
snowy: It's snowy. Il neige.
soup soupe f
spider araignée f
sponge cake madeleine f
spoon cuillère f
square carré m
stairs l'escalier m
stand up: I stand up. Je me lève.
star étoile f
starfish étoile de mer f
steak steak m
stormy: It's stormy. Il y a de
    l'orage.
straw paille f
strawberry fraise f
strong fort
sugar sucre m
sun soleil m
sun hat chapeau de soleil m
sunglasses lunettes de soleil f
sunny: It's sunny. Il fait soleil.
supermarket supermarché m
sweatshirt sweat m
sweets bonbons m
swimming pool piscine f

swimming trunks caleçon m sing
swimsuit maillot de bain m
swing balançoire ƒ

T, t

table table ƒ
tambourine tambourin m
tea thé m
teacher maîtresse ƒ
teddy bear ours en peluche m
teeth dents ƒ; I brush my teeth.
    Je me brosse les dents.
ten dix
thirsty: I'm thirsty. J'ai soif.
three trois
tiger tigre m
tired: I'm tired. Je suis fatiguée.
toast tartine grillée ƒ
toe doigt de pied m
toilet: I go to the toilet. Je vais
    aux toilettes.
tomato tomate ƒ
toothbrush brosse à dents ƒ
toothpaste dentifrice m
tortoise tortue ƒ
touch: I touch my toes. Je touche
    mes orteils.
towel serviette ƒ
town ville ƒ
toy box coffre à jouets m
toy shop magasin de jouets m
toys jouets m
train train m
tree arbre m
triangle triangle m
trousers pantalon m sing
trumpet trompette ƒ
T-shirt tee-shirt m

tummy ventre m
tuna sandwich sandwich au
    thon m
turtle tortue de mer ƒ
two deux

U, u

umbrella parapluie m

V, v

violin violon m

W, w

walk: I walk. Je marche.
walrus morse m
wash: I wash my hands. Je me
    lave les mains.
water eau ƒ
watermelon pastèque ƒ
wave: I wave. Je fais un signe
    de la main.
weak faible
weather temps m
whale baleine ƒ
whisk fouet m
white blanc
whiteboard tableau m
windy: It's windy. Il fait du vent.

X, x

xylophone xylophone m

Y, y

yellow jaune
yoghurt yaourt m

Z, z

zebra zèbre m